Abigail Rae, this one is for you.
CS

To Poppy, Joey, Freddie, and Lucy
TH

First US edition 2021

Library of Congress Catalog Card Number pending
ISBN 978-1-5362-1519-9

TLF 26 25 24 23 22 21
10 9 8 7 6 5 4 3 2 1

Printed in Dongguan, Guangdong, China

This book was typeset in Brioso Pro and Gararond.
The illustrations were done in oil.

Candlewick Press
99 Dover Street
Somerville, Massachusetts 02144

www.candlewick.com

KOOKABURRA

CLAIRE SAXBY

ILLUSTRATED BY
TANNYA HARRICKS

CANDLEWICK PRESS

In the crinkled shadows,
night dwellers yawn,
day creatures stretch,
and Kookaburra laughs.

In a line on a limb with her mate and
three young, she leads a sunrise chorus.

Kook-kook-kook.

Kak-kak-kak.

When they are done, her family members leave,
each on a solo search for food.

Kookaburra stays.

She tips her head to the side,
watches,
watches,
straightens,
watches.

Swoops!

Kookaburras have very good eyesight, and tipping their head to the side helps them spot their prey more easily.

Her mate appears, a skink in his beak.
It is a gift for Kookaburra as they
approach a new nesting season.

Together they go nest hunting.
She *kookas*,
he *kookas*,
soft murmurings for their ears only.

Kookaburras mostly partner for life but still court before each nesting season.

7

Kookaburra and her
mate flit from tree to
tree in search of the
perfect hollow.

She peeks;
he peeks.

Too small.

Too low.

8

Not right.

They return to
a familiar tree
hollow—last
year's nest.
It's perfect.

*Each year, pairs look for
a new nesting hollow,
but 50 percent of the
time, they use the nest
from the previous year.*

Kook-kook-kook. Kak-kak-kak.

Kookaburra listens.
It is not her family. It is the call of strangers.
She must act.

Kookaburra families
have established
territories and
defend their borders.

In a line on a limb
with her family, her mate,
Kookaburra laughs.

Kook-kook-kook.
Kak-kak-kak.

Across the river that separates them,
the other family laughs again.
It is a challenge.

*Territorial displays become more
frequent as nesting season approaches.*

Kookaburra flies a high circle over the opposition territory. A kookaburra from beyond the river circles Kookaburra's territory.

Kookaburra's mate flies toward a tree, flares his feathers
at the mouth of a hollow, then returns to sit alongside her.

A neighbor mirrors his flight.

*These rituals confirm territory boundaries
without the need for fighting. It's as if
the birds are saying, "This is our place."*

The songs dwindle.
Their boundaries are safe for now.
And it's lunchtime.
Again, Kookaburra sits alone.
There will be snails here.

She watches and swoops.
Thwack,
   thwack—she cracks a shell and swallows.
She returns to the nesting hollow to check that
it is ready for the eggs that she will soon lay.

*Female kookaburras are larger than
males and need more food, particularly
in preparation for laying eggs.*

Her mate is nearby. He comes
and goes, bringing a cricket, then a worm.

She **kookas**.

He **kookas**.

A single kookaburra appears. This is an invasion.
Kookaburra's family attacks, fast and fierce.
The invader flees.
Nesting is a tense time, and everyone works
together to make sure it goes well.

*Single kookaburras sometimes invade other
territories in search of a mate. Unless one
of a pair has died, there is no vacancy.*

As day drifts into evening, Kookaburra gathers her family.

Soon she will lay her eggs.

While she sits on them, Kookaburra's family will bring food, protect their territory, and sometimes share the nesting.

Kookaburras usually lay three eggs at a time. They are dull white and about the size of golf balls. Kookaburra families mostly roost close together.

21

Once the chicks are hatched, the family will share
the tasks of feeding, teaching, and raising them.

But not today. Today Kookaburra
leads the night song.

This twilight, in a line on a limb
with her family, her mate,
Kookaburra laughs.

Kook-kook-kook.

Kak-kak-kak.

More About Kookaburras

The laughing kookaburra is the larger of the two Australian kookaburra species. Both are part of the kingfisher family. The name *kookaburra* is an adaptation of an Aboriginal word and describes their song. The laughing kookaburra is found widely throughout the eastern parts of Australia and in southern South Australia and Western Australia. They live where there is permanent access to water, food, and nesting sites. Their diet consists mostly of insects, spiders, and small reptiles. Laughing kookaburras have distinctive eye stripes, which can help them identify family members and intruders. Young kookaburras have a dark lower beak, which becomes lighter as they mature. They sometimes stay for a few years before leaving the family to find their own partners. Kookaburras mostly nest in tree hollows but have been known to nest in termite mounds and haystacks. They are adaptable and may live close to humans.

Index

Look up the pages to find out about all these kookaburra things.
Don't forget to look at both kinds of words—this kind and this kind.